Greenwich is the reference point for the world's time. It is to C
on earth looks to set their watches.

But this leafy London town, where the eastern and western hemispheres meet at
longitude zero, is home to more than abstract concepts about time and space. The town of
Greenwich is part of a much larger borough, brimming with all the usual economic, social
and architectural features associated with London.

After eminent royal and maritime beginnings, and extraordinary industrial growth, an
uncharacteristically sleepy recent history is over. Greenwich has begun to balance its pomp
and heritage with social planning and daring development.

THIS PAGE *Canaletto bathed Greenwich Hospital in the
sunlight of his native Venice when he painted this
c. 1750 view. Discounting river traffic of a very different
kind, the prospect is strikingly similar today in all but the
smallest details.*

FRONT COVER *The Queen's House and Docklands, from
Greenwich Park.*

GREENWICH AND THE THAMES

Greenwich lies at the eastern approach to London, where the River Thames sags before winding its way towards the City. Historically, anyone attacking London from Europe via Dover was forced either over Blackheath by land or past Greenwich by river.

Defence, celebration or service of the city and its river have always been key to the prosperity of the borough, which includes Blackheath, Charlton, Deptford, Eltham, Plumstead and Woolwich, together with Greenwich itself.

Each is close enough to central London to feed off the wealth of the city, while far enough away to have its own particular characteristics.

There was a time when the Thames was crowded with shipping and cargo from all over the world, making the riverside temporarily the most prosperous on earth.

Occasionally the mud of the area throws up some shard of London's hidden past. The construction site of Greenwich's brave new future has revealed some clues about the area's ancient inhabitants. As yet there is no proof that anyone lived along this once marshy stretch of the Thames before the Romans came to Britain – and they probably did not live here either. Roman relics dug up in Greenwich in 1902 are thought to have come from an isolated temple, situated on the way to Londinium, which the Romans had established upriver by AD 43.

By the 2nd century, flat-bottomed barges were regularly carrying loads into Londinium – a sign of the traffic to come. The next invaders were the Saxons, in the 6th century. The first real proof of any settlers in Greenwich comes in the 10th century, when it is recorded that the Saxon king Edgar gave part of his property in the area to the abbey of Ghent. The hugely complicated saga of the ownership and development of this ancient property, which is partly defined today

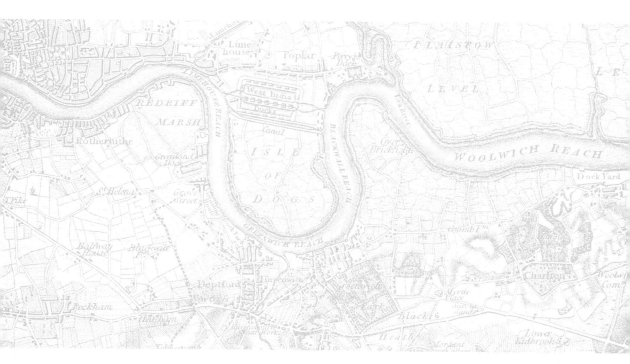

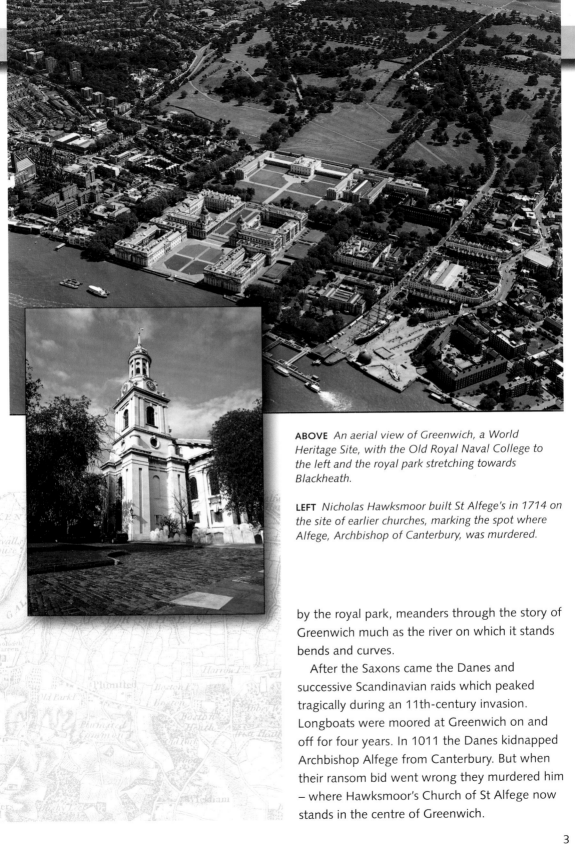

ABOVE *An aerial view of Greenwich, a World Heritage Site, with the Old Royal Naval College to the left and the royal park stretching towards Blackheath.*

LEFT *Nicholas Hawksmoor built St Alfege's in 1714 on the site of earlier churches, marking the spot where Alfege, Archbishop of Canterbury, was murdered.*

by the royal park, meanders through the story of Greenwich much as the river on which it stands bends and curves.

After the Saxons came the Danes and successive Scandinavian raids which peaked tragically during an 11th-century invasion. Longboats were moored at Greenwich on and off for four years. In 1011 the Danes kidnapped Archbishop Alfege from Canterbury. But when their ransom bid went wrong they murdered him – where Hawksmoor's Church of St Alfege now stands in the centre of Greenwich.

By the 16th century much naval shipbuilding was taking place along the banks of the Thames, with royal dockyards at Deptford and downriver at Woolwich. In 1514 Henry VIII launched his flagship, the *Henri Grace à Dieu*, at Woolwich. She was the largest ship in the largest navy England had ever seen. Henry's new, more powerful navy strengthened the defence of England's coasts and added to the king's prestige. This stretch of the Thames continued to produce most of Britain's warships until 1869.

The days of England's naval supremacy had their ceremonial peak with the funeral of her most famous admiral, Lord Nelson, after his defeat of the French at Trafalgar. On Christmas Day 1805 his body was carried ashore at Greenwich Hospital – now the Old Royal Naval College – in readiness for the three-day lying-in-state in the Painted Hall.

LEFT *Sir Peter Lely's portrait of Peter Pett, the master shipwright at the Royal Dockyard, Woolwich, where the famous vessel Sovereign of the Seas was constructed in 1637. Pepys, the diarist, described the ship as 'a glorious vessel . . . being for defence and ornament the richest that ever spread cloth before the wind'.*

Tens of thousands of people clogged Greenwich for days, desperate to pay their respects. All shipping was cleared from the river to allow the fabulous flotilla of gilt barges with ceremonial flags to accompany the body upstream to St Paul's Cathedral for the funeral and burial in the crypt.

Turner's famous painting *The Fighting Téméraire*, sketched near Greenwich in 1838, shows a different type of funeral. Steam belches into the sky from a little iron tug as it tows the ghostly old wooden man-of-war to the breaker's yard. By this time wood and sail were giving way to iron and steam, increasingly forcing shipbuilding into the north where the raw materials were. The naval yards at Woolwich and Deptford closed in 1869. The last Thames-built Royal Navy ship, HMS *Thunderer*, was launched across the river from Greenwich at Bow Creek in 1912.

ABOVE *William Parrott's 1841 view of the Dreadnought, a hospital ship moored upstream from Greenwich Hospital. Disabled merchant seamen of all nationalities were cared for on the massive hulk.*

RIGHT *L.F. Abbott's portrait of Nelson in 1798–99 after the battle of the Nile.*

THE PALACE SAGA

The historic heart of Greenwich comprises the park, the Royal Observatory perched on its hill, and the view down to the river from there, taking in the Queen's House, the National Maritime Museum and the Old Royal Naval College. This area roughly corresponds to the estate that the Saxons had made over to the abbey of Ghent in the 10th century.

By 1433 the land was in Crown hands again and the austere abbey on the site of the present Old Royal Naval College had become the worldly Bella Court, home to Henry V's brother Humphrey, Duke of Gloucester. The duke also built a fortress on the hill, where the Royal Observatory now stands, in his newly enclosed park.

After the duke died in 1447, Bella Court was given to his nephew Henry VI's young wife, Margaret of Anjou, who changed its name to Placentia. It was later enlarged to become the enormous, castellated Greenwich Palace that dominated the river for 160 years.

Henry VIII was born here and grew to love the place, especially for its elaborate parties, hunting and gallant jousting tournaments. This gallantry, however, did not prevent him replacing his wife, Catherine of Aragon, with Anne Boleyn, whose daughter, later Elizabeth I, was also born here.

RIGHT *Elizabeth I at the time of the threatened Spanish invasion. In August 1588 she travelled from Greenwich to Tilbury to review her armada troops and make her famous rallying speech.*

ABOVE *Greenwich Palace from the river, from an early 17th-century painting.*

Elizabeth I loved Greenwich Palace, from where she could gaze at the river, watching the world go by – or at least watching explorers go by – on their way to find out what the world looked like. Martin Frobisher sailed past here to look for the Northwest Passage; and it was on the *Golden Hind* at Greenwich that Queen Elizabeth awarded Sir Francis Drake a knighthood after he had circumnavigated the globe. Greenwich may also have been the place where Sir Walter Raleigh famously laid his cloak down over a puddle for the Virgin Queen to walk on.

BELOW *Johannes Vorsterman's 1676 view of Greenwich shows the Tudor palace in ruins and the Queen's House enjoying an uninterrupted view of the Thames for the first time. The west wing of Charles II's abandoned 'King's House' was later rescued and became part of the Royal Naval College.*

BOTTOM *Charles II intended to replace Greenwich Palace but work stopped in 1665. Queen Mary II asked Christopher Wren to complete the buildings as a hospital for veteran sailors, insisting that the grand vista from the Queen's House to the river should not be impeded. The Naval College's 125-year occupancy began in 1873.*

THE QUEEN'S HOUSE

One of Greenwich's headiest eras ended in 1603 with the death of Queen Elizabeth I, and the royal estate was largely neglected until James I gave it to his queen, Anne of Denmark. It was for her that Inigo Jones began to build the architecturally radical Queen's House, although she died in 1619, before it was finished.

By the time the Queen's House was nearing completion in 1635, Charles I was on the throne, but his wife, Henrietta Maria, was unable to enjoy the house before the Civil War drove her into exile in France. During Cromwell's Commonwealth, the Queen's House fared better than the palace, which was turned first into a barracks and then later a biscuit factory.

Charles II returned from France after the restoration of the monarchy with plans to rebuild Greenwich Palace. But the Great Plague in 1665 put paid to his scheme. He lost interest and his new 'King's House', only partly finished, languished until it was incorporated into the Greenwich Hospital.

But Charles did at least realise one new and far-reaching dream – an observatory on the hill. Henrietta Maria, now the Queen Mother, returned briefly to live in the Queen's House before her death in France in 1669.

RIGHT *Doors leading to the black and white marble loggia from where visitors to the Queen's House can take in a splendid view of the park and the Old Royal Observatory on the hill.*

BELOW *The Great Hall, a perfect cube, has a marble floor and an intricately carved wooden balustrade. The ceiling is a copy of the Gentileschi original, removed to Marlborough House in London in the 18th century.*

FAR LEFT *The open-well 'Tulip' staircase, the first of its kind in England. The spiralling stone steps lead to a skylight in the roof.*

LEFT *Henrietta Maria by Sir Anthony van Dyck. Before she went into exile in 1644 Henrietta Maria had ordered furnishings and paintings for her 'house of delight', which she enjoyed after her return in 1660.*

LEFT *Inigo Jones, the designer of the Queen's House. William Hogarth's portrait was modelled on a drawing by van Dyck.*

– THE QUEEN'S HOUSE –

The Queen's House, the first classical domestic house in England, was inspired by the Italian villas of Andrea Palladio. It is now part of the National Maritime Museum.

The new palace began to decay and might have disappeared altogether after William and Mary came to the throne in 1689, had it not been for another royal enthusiasm: the idea of building a hospital for veteran sailors. Queen Mary made this the 'darling object of her life', but died of smallpox in 1694 before seeing it realised. Sir Christopher Wren, supported by Sir John Vanbrugh and Nicholas Hawksmoor, turned her dream into London's greatest example of the grand English baroque style.

The 42 disabled men who limped into the colossus when it opened in 1705 must have felt distinctly overshadowed. Numbers slowly increased to a total of 3,000. But by 1850 most of the sailors of Nelson's era were dead, and progressively fewer veterans needed or wanted the spartan conditions hidden behind the opulent façades. The hospital closed in 1869, the same year as the Woolwich Dockyard.

In 1873 the Royal Naval College took over the buildings, and the chapel and magnificent Painted Hall were opened to the public. The Royal Navy remained until 1998 but the educational function of the site continues as students of the University of Greenwich and of Trinity College of Music now occupy the buildings.

The most recent development is the Discover Greenwich exhibition in Pepys House. Centred around a spectacular model of the Maritime Greenwich World Heritage Site, this free exhibition explores over 500 years of Greenwich history from Tudor times to the present day. The building is also home to Greenwich Tourist Information Centre and the wonderful Old Brewery restaurant and bar.

RIGHT *Wren's chapel was rebuilt by James 'Athenian' Stuart after a fire in 1779. The altar painting is by Benjamin West.*

THE OLD ROYAL NAVAL COLLEGE

BELOW *Dr Samuel Johnson considered Greenwich Hospital 'far too magnificent for a place of charity'. Soon after the last elderly sailors departed in 1869, the buildings became the Royal Naval College.*

ABOVE *James Thornhill took 19 years to paint allegorical scenes on the ceilings and walls of the magnificent Painted Hall.*

ABOVE *An interactive map of the Maritime Greenwich World Heritage Site at the Discover Greenwich exhibition centre.*

THE NATIONAL MARITIME MUSEUM

The National Maritime Museum was founded in 1934. It is a spectacular celebration of Great Britain, Greenwich and the sea. The Royal Observatory Greenwich and the Queen's House, two of the finest buildings in the country, are part of the museum, but the real focus of the enormous maritime collection (there are over two million items in all) is the complex of galleries joined by a colonnade to the Queen's House. This west wing, and a similar one to the east of the house, were both built after the Queen's House became a school for the children of seamen in 1806.

All the museum's buildings have been upgraded at various times since it opened and the last major redevelopment of Neptune Court, with its huge glazed roof, was completed in 1999. The latest addition to the museum, however, is the dazzling Sammy Ofer Wing which, with its custom-built exhibition spaces and highly accessible archives, marks a major change in the way the museum's collections

and programmes are presented to the public. The museum holds a comprehensive range of artefacts chronicling the history of Britain at sea, covering everything from navigation to exploration. Nelson's extraordinary life is given due prominence with objects from his career on display, including the uniform coat that he wore when he was fatally wounded at the Battle of Trafalgar in 1805.

The museum takes its visitors on a voyage through maritime history from far-off times right up to the present day. The maritime galleries explore Britain's encounters with the world at sea from the 16th to the early 20th centuries. Visitors can hear the story of human exploration, learn about waves and tides, see how our lives depend on the ocean and even steer a ship into port. In addition, the museum houses an impressive collection of maritime art, including British and 17th-century Dutch artists. There are also interactive displays in the All Hands and The Bridge galleries aimed at bringing maritime history to life for children. The outstanding permanent and temporary exhibitions in the Sammy Ofer Wing can only underline the institution's reputation as probably the finest maritime museum in the world.

LEFT *The ornately decorated state barge of Frederick, Prince of Wales, eldest son of George II. It is one of several elaborate barges in the museum.*

RIGHT *Charles II founded the Old Royal Observatory for navigational research in 1675.*

BELOW *The Upper Deck at the National Maritime Museum is just one of several spacious exhibition areas.*

PIVOT OF THE WORLD

Greenwich stands on the prime meridian, the imaginary line running between the north and south poles, from which all other longitudinal lines spread east and west to divide the globe into measurable segments over which the sun passes at regular intervals. The use of Greenwich for this purpose derives from Charles II's shrewd decision to build an observatory here in 1675. Again, the impetus came from the river and the sea.

Ships that left London to conquer or trade abroad needed better navigation: mapping out longitude was a way to achieve this. Charles was advised that this would be best done by observing the moon and the stars over a long period. So Christopher Wren designed an observatory which would not merely be efficient but would have appropriate 'pompe' for the important task in hand.

This task fell to John Flamsteed, the first Astronomer Royal, who battled with poor wages and ill health for over 40 years to make over 50,000 observations. His *Historia Coelestis Britannica* was posthumously published in 1725, and without it the prime meridian would never have ended up at Greenwich.

But the man who finally worked out how to find longitude at sea was a Yorkshire-born clockmaker, John Harrison, who worked with Flamsteed's successor, Edmond Halley, to develop a very special and advanced form of sea clock. Regardless of temperature changes at sea, his chronometer would always tell the right time.

The problem had been that the position of the sun at any given time varies around the world, so one person's midday would not be another's. The trick was to know your local time from the sun and its difference from the fixed prime meridian; then your longitude could be calculated. A prime meridian had to be set. Where was this to be?

At a conference in Washington DC in 1884 a majority of delegates from 25 nations decided that the world's prime meridian should be at Greenwich. This was not in deference to the gruelling groundwork done by Flamsteed, but purely pragmatic recognition that by then 72 per cent of world commerce and, most importantly, the United States of America, already used Greenwich to set their clocks by.

ABOVE *The prime meridian line – longitude zero – runs between the north and south poles. Its position in Greenwich is shown by the line across the observatory courtyard.*

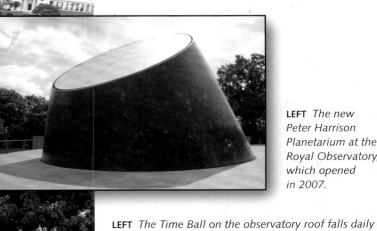

LEFT *The new Peter Harrison Planetarium at the Royal Observatory, which opened in 2007.*

LEFT *The Time Ball on the observatory roof falls daily at 1300 hours, and in the days of sail it gave ships on the river a visual time check. On the wall by the gates is the 24-hour clock which has displayed Greenwich time for over a century.*

AN INSPIRATION TO DICKENS

The first literary mention of London, in AD 61 by Tacitus, described it as being crowded with merchants and trading ships. Over many centuries the momentum did not let up, and by the time the *Téméraire* was broken up in 1838, shipyards were giving way to docks that, together with the wharves and factories, serviced an enormous expansion of trade and industry.

The waterfront had to adapt to the changing times. For example, manufacture of ropes at the Enderby factory in Greenwich switched to electric cables after the buildings burned down in 1845. The cables produced were later uncoiled over the ocean floors from ships that left here to unleash the first great wave of electronic communication.

Shipbuilding still continued in nearby dockyards – mainly steel barges that joined the motley mixture of wood, iron, steam and sail-powered clippers, like the *Cutty Sark*, that clogged the river, fetching and carrying goods from around the globe.

Small terraced houses and the pubs that served the inhabitants proliferated by the river as Greenwich grew into a melting pot of rich and poor. Charles Dickens, a regular of the Trafalgar Tavern, drew inspiration from the urban scene, making its characters famous throughout the world.

RIGHT *The Cutty Sark before the conservation process began. The ship will reopen in 2012, revived and ready for a new generation of visitors.*

INSET RIGHT *The Cutty Sark's figurehead is the bewitched heroine of Robert Burns's poem Tam o'Shanter. She wears a woollen shift or 'cutty sark' and clutches at the horse's tail, as in the legend.*

ABOVE *Visitors have been arriving in Greenwich by river for centuries. River boats and fast Thames Clipper catamarans still operate daily and at frequent intervals.*

LEFT *Charles Dickens used the Trafalgar Tavern as background for an episode in Our Mutual Friend. The tavern was also popular with other famous writers and artists.*

– THE CUTTY SARK –

The *Cutty Sark*'s great keel was placed on a concrete plinth at Greenwich in 1954. But from the clipper's launch in 1869 until 1895 this keel sliced through the world's oceans at record-breaking speeds, carrying tea from China and, later, wool from Australia. Even as clippers go the *Cutty Sark* was always one of the most beautiful, but the coming of steam increasingly took the wind out of her sails and in 1895 she was sold to a Portuguese company. The year before, she had been seen at full speed by a young Cornish sailor, Wilfred Dowman. He was so inspired by the sight that, 28 years later, seeing the *Cutty Sark* in a dilapidated state, he bought and restored her. From 1923 until after the Second World War she was a nautical training ship. In November 2006 she closed to the public in order to undergo conservation work. A fire broke out in the hull on 21 May 2007 but fortunately many parts of the ship were away being renovated at the time. The *Cutty Sark* Trust is determined that she will once again be restored to her former glory. She is due to re-open in 2012.

AN END AND A BEGINNING

In spite of growing competition from the north of England and abroad, and disruption during the First World War, Thames trade continued to boom until the depression of 1929. The subsequent slow recovery was then checked by the devastation of the Second World War. In September 1940 German planes tried to bomb the docklands north of the river into oblivion. The Woolwich ferry ran all night evacuating people to south of the river.

But after the war the river traffic revived, and in 1964 wharves and warehouses handled 61 million tons of cargo – a figure never to be exceeded.

Then, with astonishing suddenness, London's life as an international port vanished. Container shipping and roll-on roll-off ferries made this stretch of the Thames redundant. The new container dock 26 miles away at Tilbury had better motorway and rail access, and unrestricted sites. The change sucked much of the life out of east London, abandoning the people who had lived and worked there to pick up the pieces. The last London dock closed in 1981.

Since then, substantial redevelopment has taken place across the river from Greenwich on the Isle of Dogs, where a cluster of some of London's newest buildings stare back at one of London's oldest, the Royal Observatory. Dominated by One Canada Square – from 1991 to 2010 the tallest building in the UK – the development in and around Canary Wharf is now home to many of the country's newspapers, the Museum of London Docklands, and a thriving business district with a wide range of shops, restaurants, pubs and bars.

RIGHT *Admiral Lord Nelson stands watch outside the Trafalgar Tavern on the banks of the River Thames.*

– THE THAMES BARRIER –

High tide on the Thames is immensely powerful, twice daily sweeping in from the North Sea at 100 metres per minute. A flood in central London would be devastating: the Thames Barrier was built to prevent it ever happening. The barrier took ten years from 1974 to build and cost some £500 million. The largest of the great retractable gates between the gleaming piers each weigh over 5,000 tonnes.

LEFT *Baroque meets modern as the sparkling towers of Canary Wharf and London's docklands loom amiably over the elegant façades of the Queen's House and the Old Royal Naval College.*

RIGHT *Students relax in the grounds of the Old Royal Naval College as The O2 gleams in the sun.*

A GROWING ELEGANCE

By the 17th century, Greenwich town was already of considerable size and wealth, and Crooms Hill – one of the oldest roads in London – along the west side of the park, had always been one of the most prosperous streets. The Ranger's House, at the top of the hill, is an elegant Georgian villa which now houses the remarkable Wernher Collection of works of art amassed by diamond magnate Sir Julius Wernher. At around the same period Nicholas Hawksmoor built the imposing classical Church of St Alfege at the bottom of the hill. From here the town centre, including the well-known Arts and Crafts Market, is largely defined by a Regency new town plan, designed by Joseph Kay between 1829 and 1843. The famous Trafalgar Tavern (built in 1837), by the river east of the Old Royal Naval College, is one of Kay's creations. Charles Dickens was just one of the 'in crowd' who liked it here.

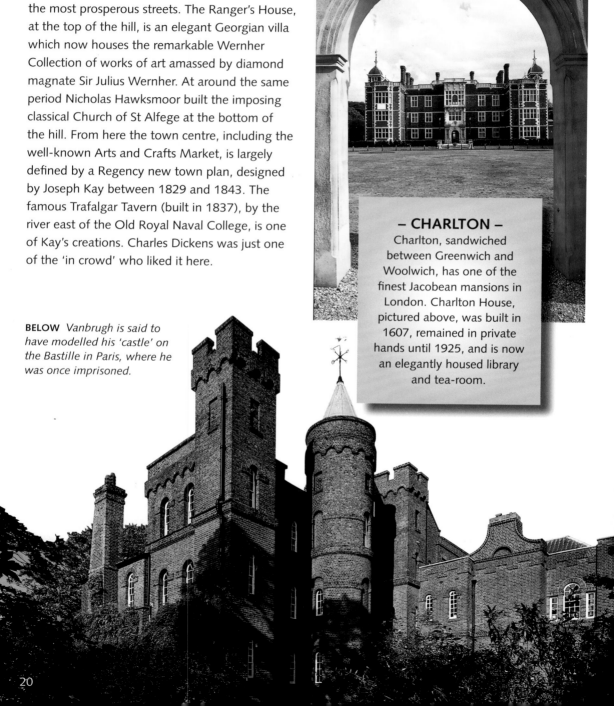

BELOW *Vanbrugh is said to have modelled his 'castle' on the Bastille in Paris, where he was once imprisoned.*

– CHARLTON –
Charlton, sandwiched between Greenwich and Woolwich, has one of the finest Jacobean mansions in London. Charlton House, pictured above, was built in 1607, remained in private hands until 1925, and is now an elegantly housed library and tea-room.

RIGHT *The Ranger's House (1699) is home to an impressive array of Jacobean portraits.*

FAR RIGHT *Firepower, The Royal Artillery Museum, is one of the world's oldest military museums. It is located next to Greenwich Heritage Centre in the historic Royal Arsenal, Woolwich, by the side of the River Thames.*

West of the college, where the soon-to-be completed *Cutty Sark* now stands, the riverside was once a confused sprawl of lanes serving the busy river. East of the Trafalgar Tavern things were slightly grander. One fine early building that still stands is the Trinity Hospital, opened in 1614 and rebuilt in 1812. Further east, towards the Greenwich Peninsula, the typically confident home of the 19th-century Enderby family will soon become part of a brand-new cruise liner terminal. Sir John Vanbrugh, who helped design the Greenwich Hospital, built himself Vanbrugh Castle east of Greenwich Park on Maze Hill in 1719. This grim romantic folly was restored in 1977. Up and over the hill on the other side of Blackheath, Sir John Morden, who made his fortune in shipping, used an existing estate in 1695 to found an influential philanthropic charity to house elderly shipping merchants. In the 19th century his Morden College became one of Greenwich's main developers. Many of the small terraced houses, built at that time to house the influx of new workers, still bear the mark 'MC 1695'.

– THE FAN MUSEUM –

In two beautifully restored early Georgian houses on Crooms Hill is the world's only museum devoted to the art and craft of the fan. Besides the permanent collection of this charming fashion accessory from a bygone age, there are regular changing exhibitions, an orangery and a small Japanese garden.

MODERN DEVELOPMENTS

Greenwich's 20th-century development has both scarred and enhanced the borough. In 1902 the ferry across the Thames from Cutty Sark Gardens to the Isle of Dogs was replaced by the Greenwich Foot Tunnel, lined with 200,000 tiles. In the same year, building began on a new power station – controversially close to the ancient Trinity Hospital – which purists appreciate for its interesting mixture of Edwardian 'church Gothic' and industrial functionalism. The four chimneys should have been higher, but the Astronomer Royal said the smoke would 'obscure the heavens'.

Bombs and town improvements have removed most of the riverside's dark alleys, but not everything that has replaced them has been particularly imaginative.

Perhaps the most controversial development since the Second World War was the Millennium

FAR LEFT *An unusual waterspout contemplates its surroundings at the Old Royal Naval College.*

LEFT *The main guardhouse at the entrance to the Royal Arsenal, Woolwich. The arsenal contains many historic buildings, some of which will form part of a planned heritage centre.*

Dome on Greenwich Peninsula. Built to celebrate the start of the new millennium, the Dome was home to a vast exhibition and performance space throughout 2000. Even though it attracted over 6.5 million visitors, the Dome was perceived as a failure and, after the exhibition closed, it stood empty for nearly seven years.

It re-opened as The O2 in June 2007 with a concert featuring Bon Jovi. The 22,000-seat arena inside The O2 instantly attracted big names in music, sport and comedy, and rapidly became – and remains – one of the most popular entertainment venues in the world. Greenwich Peninsula is now also home to the architecturally striking Ravensbourne, the Greenwich Millennium Village and an increasing number of attractive, new business-oriented buildings.

BELOW *Trinity Hospital was founded as almshouses by the Earl of Northampton in 1614, and his effigy is an imposing feature of the chapel. It gained its crenellated parapets in a 19th-century neo-Gothic restoration. The Mercers' Company still selects 20 pensioners to live here.*

– ELTHAM –

Eltham is home to an astonishing architectural hybrid: the country's most extravagant 1930s house has been grafted onto the remains of a medieval palace. Eltham Palace was first used as a royal residence in 1311, gradually evolving until the Tudor Greenwich Palace began to eclipse it. Following the Civil War, Eltham slowly decayed and the magnificent 15th-century Great Hall became a barn, painted by Turner in 1790. In 1933 the millionaire Stephen Courtauld and his wife Virginia were allowed to demolish the ruined Victorian additions to build a country house, on the condition that they restored the Great Hall. Over the next four years they created a sumptuous monument to the Modern Movement with the splendid Great Hall at one end.

THE PURSUIT OF PLEASURE

The pomp of Greenwich's high architecture conceals an otherwise typically dockside proletarian past, with a big working-class electorate. William Gladstone appealed to these people for help in 1868 when he needed a new constituency from which to fight the Tories. After a mass meeting on Blackheath, the town adopted him. As the new prime minister, Gladstone and his liberal supporters became regulars at the Trafalgar Tavern's famous whitebait suppers.

The heath has a history of massed rallies in support of radical causes. Yet hedonism has regularly brought the population out in force too. Almost as soon as the public were allowed into Greenwich Park in the 18th century, some people began to lose control. An early craze was the sometimes dangerous pastime of 'tumbling' (throwing yourself down a hill). Rowdy 'out-of-towners' soon got the bug, and by the 1840s this rough and tumbling had grown into the vast Greenwich Fair which attracted as many as 150,000 people. When it was abolished in 1857 the crowds simply walked up the hill to Blackheath Fair.

BELOW *Enjoying Greenwich Park – the Queen's House and the Old Royal Naval College are in the background.*

BELOW *The boating lake and playground at the foot of Greenwich Park are popular with families during the summer. An ornamental lake with wildfowl lies on higher ground in the park.*

RIGHT AND BELOW *Oxleas Wood, the only survivor of south-east London's medieval forests, is a haven for wildlife. A deer grazes in the wilderness in Greenwich Park; it would be nice to think it was a descendant of the original herd introduced by Henry VIII in 1535.*

LEFT *The Royal Observatory has witnessed all sorts of shenanigans over the years.*

– BLACKHEATH –

Blackheath has often been at the centre of historical events. In 1381 Wat Tyler gathered more than 100,000 people here to protest against the poll tax. In 1415 Henry V returned from Agincourt to be congratulated by 20,000 Londoners on the heath. In 1497 another tax riot, this time by Cornishmen, led to a pitched battle in which about 1,000 died. In the next century Henry VIII's fourth wife, Anne of Cleves, was greeted here before she was led down to Greenwich Palace. Village life began south-east of the heath in the 1740s, given impetus by the opening of the great Morden College in 1695. Within 50 years an elegant garden suburb had emerged. It still retains its architectural variety and charm.

As far as entertainment in Greenwich goes the hugely successful O2 arena may be the biggest boy on the block, but there are plenty of other venues to go to. The splendid Greenwich Theatre was built on the site of a 19th-century music hall and is now a vibrant contemporary theatre producing its own work, and hosting quality drama and musicals from all over the country. Greenwich is also home to Up the Creek, one of London's most anarchic comedy venues, and Greenwich Playhouse, a well-regarded and long-established fringe theatre.

Greenwich Dance, housed in the old Borough Halls, produces exciting cabaret and adventurous dance, and provides a year-round programme of classes, courses and workshops. Some of the country's most talented young musicians study at Trinity Laban Conservatoire of Music and Dance, which is partly based in the Old Royal Naval College. You can hear them play regular, free recitals and concerts in St Alfege's Church, nearby Blackheath Halls and the Old Royal Naval College itself.

On top of all this, Greenwich is the venue for the Greenwich festivals throughout the year. Alongside London's biggest free arts event, the spectacular Greenwich+Docklands International Festival, there are celebrations of children's theatre, dance, jazz, a major music festival and a comedy festival (both in the grounds of the Old Royal Naval College), and even a festival dedicated to early music.

HEY DJ!

ABOVE and RIGHT As well as staging big-name music, comedy and sports events, The O2 is also home to the British Music Experience, Britain's only interactive museum of popular music.

RIGHT *St Alfege's Church hosts hundreds of free recitals and concerts every year.*

FAR RIGHT *Greenwich Theatre is a lively contemporary venue which started life as a music hall.*

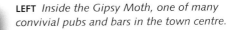

LEFT *Inside the Gipsy Moth, one of many convivial pubs and bars in the town centre.*

BELOW *The Greenwich+Docklands International Festival kicks off a series of events each summer featuring music, jazz, dance, comedy and park events, all under the banner of the Greenwich Festivals.*

LOOKING AHEAD

Over the next few years Greenwich sees the completion of many long-term projects and the arrival of the biggest sporting event in the world: the London 2012 Olympic and Paralympic Games. The Borough of Greenwich is an Olympic venue with three separate sites staging events in 12 sports. Events take place at Woolwich Barracks, North Greenwich Arena (The O2) and Greenwich Park, which hosts the equestrian events and elements of the modern pentathlon.

Greenwich also becomes a royal borough in 2012, an honour given by Her Majesty Queen Elizabeth II in the year of her Diamond Jubilee and which recognises the borough's royal connections throughout the centuries.

Following the opening of the Sammy Ofer Wing at the National Maritime Museum, 2012 sees the long-awaited completion of the renovation work on the *Cutty Sark*. Cutty Sark Gardens, where the famous old ship is in dry-dock, is being extensively redesigned and the Greenwich Foot Tunnel has also been refurbished and improved.

Greenwich Pier is showing a new face as restaurants, cafes and new passenger facilities take up residence, and the entrance has been opened up to create a beautiful and unusual open space. Further downriver Greenwich becomes a truly international destination as a brand-new cruise liner terminal opens its doors at Enderby Wharf and developments on the Greenwich Peninsula continue apace.

BELOW *The evening sun shines on budding athletes in Greenwich Park.*